JOURNEY TO THE PRESIDENCY: BIOGRAPHY OF DONALD TRUMP

Children's Biography Books

BABY PROFESSOR
EDUCATION KIDS

Speedy Publishing LLC

40 E. Main St. #1156

Newark, DE 19711

www.speedypublishing.com

Copyright 2017

Donald John Trump shocked the world when he was elected as the 45th President of the United States. He first became famous as a real estate developer and businessman in New York City and later became well known as the star of "The Apprentice", a television reality show. In this book, you will be learning about his early years and how he came to be President of the United States.

CENTRAL PARK AERIAL VIEW, MANHATTAN, NEW YORK; PARK

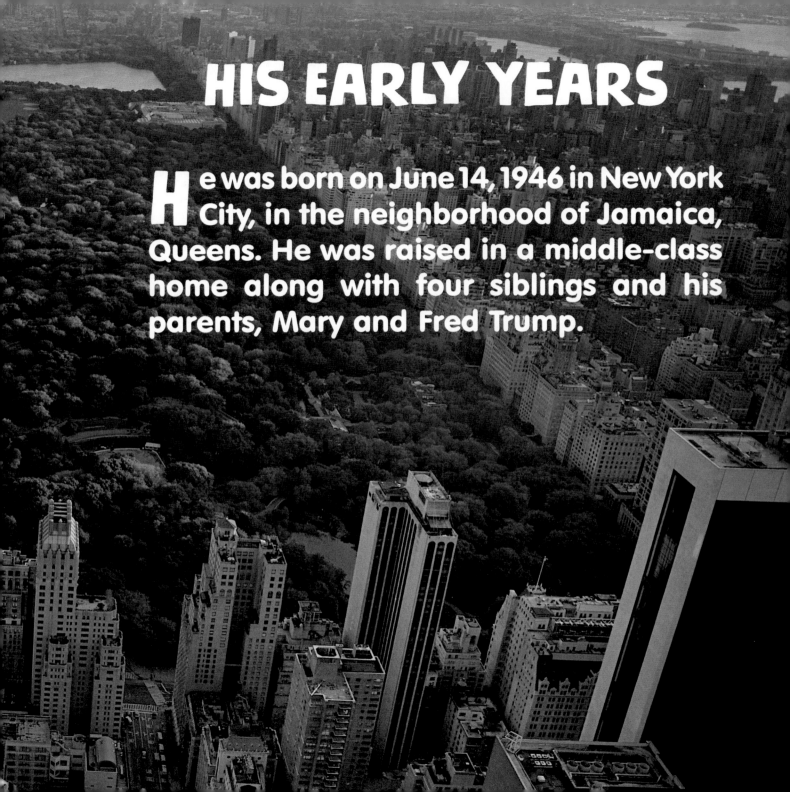

HIS EARLY YEARS

He was born on June 14, 1946 in New York City, in the neighborhood of Jamaica, Queens. He was raised in a middle-class home along with four siblings and his parents, Mary and Fred Trump.

HIS PERSONAL LIFE

He has wed three times, to Ivana Zelnickova, Marla Maples, and his current wife Melania Knauss (who is now the First Lady). He has five children, Donald Jr., Ivanka, Eric, Tiffany and Barron. His nickname is "The Donald". He also has eight grandchildren (at the time of his inauguration).

He does not indulge in alcohol since his brother, Fred Jr., passed away due to alcoholism.

DONALD AND MELANIA TRUMP

THE MILITARY ACADEMY AT WEST POINT, NEW YORK

EDUCATION

Growing up, he was full of energy and often would get into trouble at school. When he was 13, his parents had him sent to the New York Military Academy in hopes that he would become disciplined and work harder at school, and their plan worked. He became a student leader and a star athlete at the academy.

When he graduated from high school, he attended Fordham University and transferred to Wharton School of Finance, at the University of Pennsylvania, and graduated in 1968.

UNIVERSITY OF PENNSYLVANIA IN PHILADELPHIA, PENNSYLVANIA

BROOKLYN BRIDGE IN NEW YORK CITY

TRUMP'S EARLY CAREER

By the time he had graduated from college, his father, Fred Trump, was a successful real estate developer. Donald started working for his dad for the following five years in Brooklyn, New York. It was during this time that he learned quite a bit from his father about the business of real estate and how to work the deals.

REAL ESTATE DEVELOPER

One of his dreams was to be a developer of major buildings such as hotels and skyscrapers in downtown New York City. In 1976, he started his first major project when he bought the Commodore Hotel, which was very run-down, renovated it and turned it into the successful Grand Hyatt Hotel.

GRAND HYATT HOTEL

TRUMP WORLD TOWER

During the following years, Trump built and renovated skyscrapers throughout Manhattan as well as across the United States. A few of his signature buildings are the Trump International, the Trump World Tower, and the Trump Tower.

Even with his many successes, some of Trump's businesses have declared bankruptcy to reorganize and pay off debts.

THE BEAUTY PAGEANTS

Trump owned all or part of the Miss USA, Miss Universe, and Miss Teen USA beauty pageants between 1996 and 2015.

VINCE MCMAHON

WRESTLING

Trump is known to be a big WWE fan and friend of Vince McMahon, the owner of the WWE. He was the host of WrestleMania IV and WrestleMania V in 1998 and 1989 at Boardwalk Hall and has continued to be a regular participant in many of the shows. In 2013, he was inducted into the celebrity wing of the WWE Hall of Fame for his promotion contributions. The following night he had his sixth WrestleMania appearance.

REALITY TV

Trump became executive producer and host of The Apprentice, an NBC reality show, in 2003. During the show, contestants would compete for job within Trump's organization. He became known for the catchphrase "You're fired!" when a contestant was eliminated. The show became a great success. He later developed a show known as The Celebrity Apprentice which included celebrities as contestants.

During the first year, he earned $50,000 per episode (approximately $700,000 during the first season). However, following its initial success, he was earning $1 million per episode. Trump's campaign manager advised in a July 2015 press release that he was paid $213,606,575 by NBC Universal for the 14 seasons he hosted the show.

NBC announced on February 16, 2016, that they were not going to renew The Apprentice for its 15th season. Trump stated on February 27 that he didn't feel ready to sign for another season since he was thinking about running for president. After negative reaction, due to his campaign announcement speech, on June 29, NBC release a statement that said, "Due to the recent derogatory statements by Donald Trump regarding immigrants, NBC Universal is ending its business relationship with Mr. Trump."

ARNOLD SCHWARZENEGGER

DONALD TRUMP STAR HOLLYWOOD
WALK OF FAME

They replaced Trump with the actor and former Governor of California, Arnold Schwarzenegger.

In 2007, Trump was awarded with a star on the Hollywood Walk of Fame.

RUNNING FOR PRESIDENT

Donald Trump announced that he had intentions of running for president of the United States on June 16, 2015. His campaign included issues such as lowering the national debt, securing the borders, and providing work for the middle-class Americans.

MAKE
AMERICA
GREAT AGAIN!

"Make America Great Again" became his campaign slogan. He presented as the candidate that was anti-establishment and wasn't a politician and he funded personally most of his campaign.

HILLARY CLINTON

Once he won the Republican nomination, he was up against Hillary Clinton, the former Secretary of State, in the general election. It was a bitter and hard-fought election, with both nominees becoming entangled in scandals.

Once he became the presumptive Republican nominee, his focus shifted towards the general election, and he urged the remaining primary voters to "save [their] vote for the general election". He started targeting Hillary Clinton, who, on June 6, 2016, became the presumptive Democratic nominee and then continued her campaign across the country. Throughout most of 2016, Clinton had established a significant lead in the national polls.

PRESIDENTIAL DEBATE

At the beginning of July, her lead narrowed following the FBI's conclusion of the investigation into her email controversy.

Donald Trump and Hillary Clinton faced off in their first presidential debate on September 26, 2016, in Hempstead, New York at Hofstra University. The moderator was an NBC News anchor, Lester Holt. This became the most watched presidential debate in the history of the United States.

Trump went on to win the presidency on November 8, 2016, having 304 electoral votes to Clinton's 227 electoral votes. However, he won the smaller share of the popular vote and became the fifth person to win the presidency without winning the popular vote. The final popular vote difference ended up with Clinton finishing ahead by 2.1 percentage points, or 2.86 million, 48.04% to 45.95%, and neither candidate reached the majority.

3

8

3

1

7

6

55

3

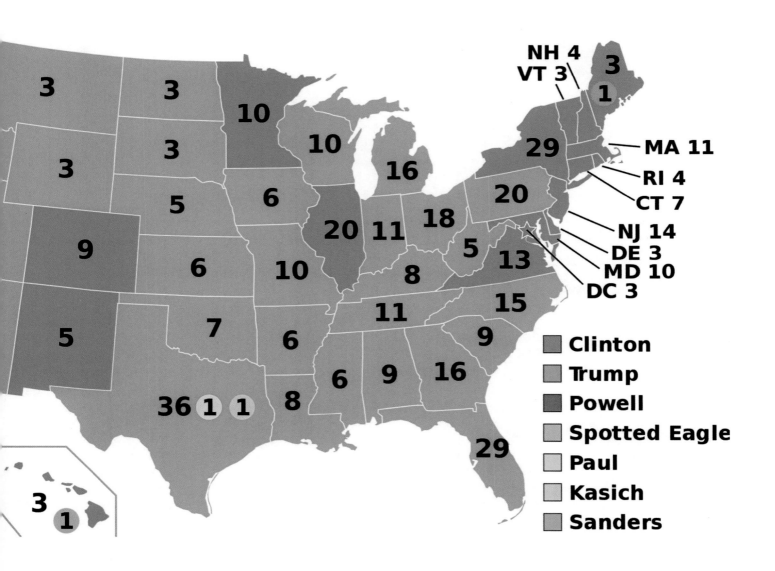

MAP OF THE ELECTORAL COLLEGE 2016 PRESIDENTIAL ELECTION RESULTS

His victory was considered to be a great political upset, since most national polls showed Clinton with a slight lead over Trump at that time, and the state polls showed her having a slight lead for winning the Electoral College. On November 9, 2016, Trump received a telephone call during the early hours in which Hillary conceded the presidency to him. He then made his victory speech in front of hundreds of supporters in New York City at the Hilton Hotel.

PRESIDENTIAL TRANSITION

When it was over, Trump had won the election and was inaugurated as president of the United States on January 20, 2017.

Chris Christie led Trump's transition team until it was taken over by Vice President-elect Mike Pence on November 11, 2016.

PRESIDENT TRUMP TAKING THE OATH OF OFFICE

DONALD TRUMP'S PRESIDENCY

Trump was sworn in by Chief Justice John G. Roberts as President of the United States on January 20, 2017 at his ceremony which took place at the United States Capitol Building. During the first hours of his presidency, he had signed many executive orders, including one to minimize "the economic burden" of the Affordable Care Act, which was also referred to as Obamacare.

On the Saturday that followed his inauguration massive demonstrations took place protesting Trump in the United States and around the world, which included the 2017 Women's March.

PROTESTERS AT TRUMP'S INAUGURATION

Trump signed the executive order on January 23, 2017 that withdraws the U.S. from the TPP (Trans-Pacific Partnership or TPPA Trans Pacific Partnership Agreement), which was a trade agreement between the U.S. and eleven Pacific Rim nations that included Vietnam, Singapore, Peru, New Zealand, Mexico, Malaysia, Japan, Chile, Canada, Brunei and Australia and would have been the beginning of a "free-trade zone for about 40 percent of the world's economy." He then ordered the building of the Mexico border wall two days later and reopened the Dakota Access and Keystone XL pipeline projects.

DAKOTA ACCESS OIL PIPELINE

MOTHER AND DAUGHTER REFUGEES

On January 27, 2017, an order that suspended admission of refugees for 120 days and also denied entry to citizens of Yemen, Syria, Sudan, Somalia, Libya, Iran and Iraq for 90 days, citing security concerns regarding terrorism. The administration later seemed to reverse part of the order, effectively exempting visitors that had a valid green card. Some federal judges issued rulings curtailing parts of the order, prohibiting the federal government from deporting visitors that were already affected.

Trump fired Acting Attorney General Sally Yates on January 30, 2017 due to her criticisms of his immigration suspension.

Trump nominated Judge Neil Gorsuch to the United States Supreme Court to replace the late Justice Antonin Scalia on January 30, 2017.

NEIL GORSUCH

MICHAEL T FLYNN

His National Security Advisor Michael T. Flynn resigned on February 13, 2017, after The Wall Street Journal reported that Flynn was being investigated by U.S. counterintelligence agents for communications with Russian officials.

February 15, two days later, Trump's Secretary of Labor nominee Andrew Puzder decided to withdraw his nomination since there was no support from either the Democrats or Republicans to confirm his nomination.

ANDREW PUZDER

PRESIDENT DONALD J. TRUMP has been quite busy since his inaugural in January of 2017 working on many other issues as well.

For additional information on President Trump, you can go to your local library, research the internet, and ask questions of your teachers, family and friends.

Made in the USA
Las Vegas, NV
19 August 2024

94077237R00040